Dedicated to all my little inspirations with
BIG imaginations: the children at Hartland International School, Dubai,
St Winefride's Catholic Primary School, Neston, UK and
Poulton Lancelyn Primary School, Bebington, UK.

Thank you to Hartland International School
for their support in creating this book.

*Charlotte Emily Jones*

Timothy Foy was an ordinary child.
A shy 6-year-old, he was quiet, not wild.

He lived happily in an old English town,
when one day, his whole life was turned upside down.

Hartland International School,
Sobha Hartland, Nad Al Sheba,
Mohammed Bin Rashid Al Maktoum City,
Dubai, United Arab Emirates

Dear Mr Foy,

Year 2 Class Teacher

We are delighted to confirm your start date of August

Mr Foy
Rose Cottage
Colchester
United Kingdom

AIRMAIL ★ AIRMAIL ★ AIRMAIL ★ AIRMAIL

A letter arrived.
Tim's dad read it with glee.
"I got the job! Here we come, UAE!"

"Yippee!" said Tim's mum,
but Tim started to worry.
"What's the UAE?
…and why all the hurry?"

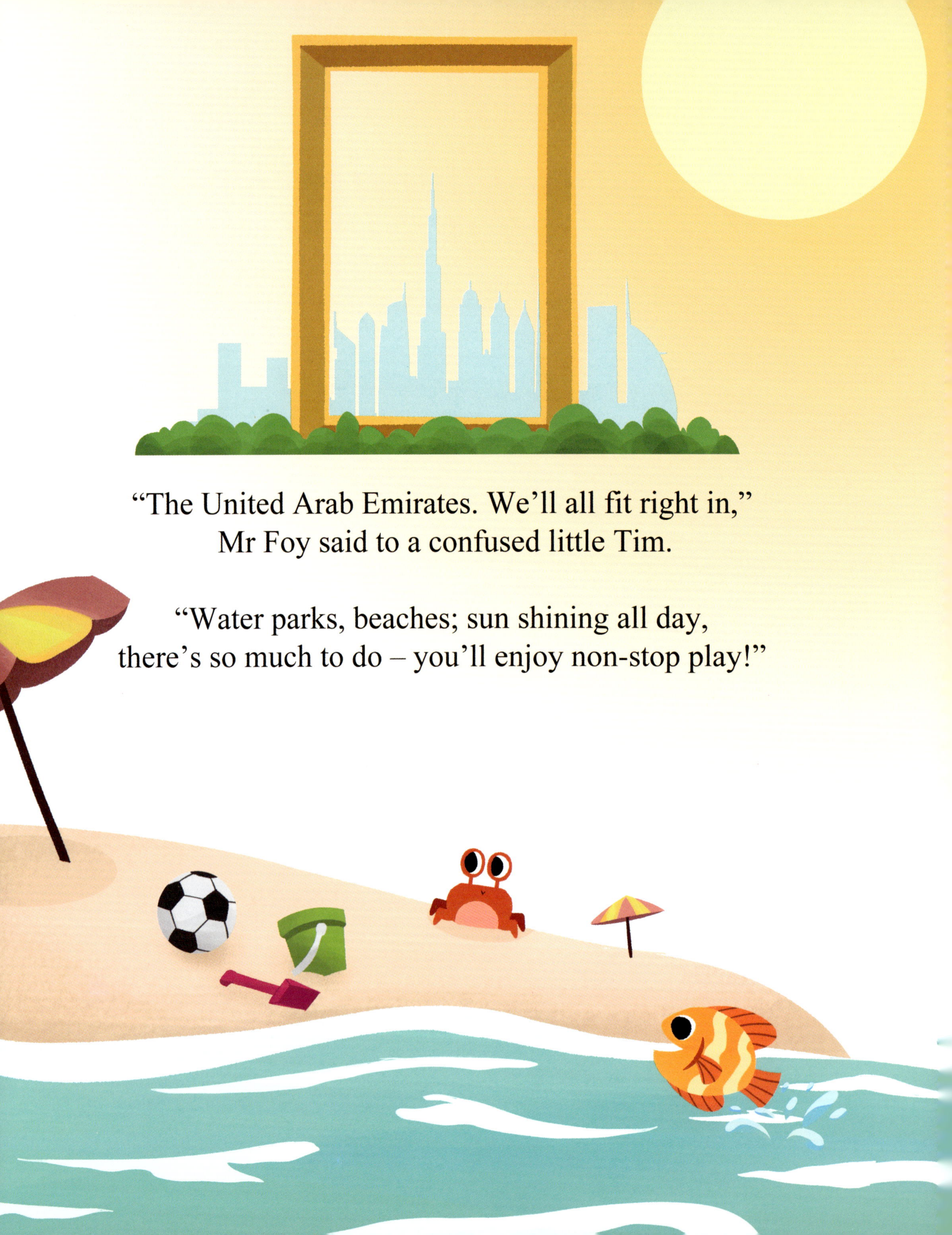

"The United Arab Emirates. We'll all fit right in,"
Mr Foy said to a confused little Tim.

"Water parks, beaches; sun shining all day,
there's so much to do – you'll enjoy non-stop play!"

Timothy pondered this tempting suggestion,
but there was still so much he wanted to question.

All of his friends,
and his school football team?
…and Nana Foy…
is she in dad's UAE dream?

Soon the time came for this sad little boy
to say bye to his friends and to pack up his toys.

“I’m going to miss you”, wailed his best friend Paul.
“Keep in touch Tim,” he said, “take our favourite ball.”

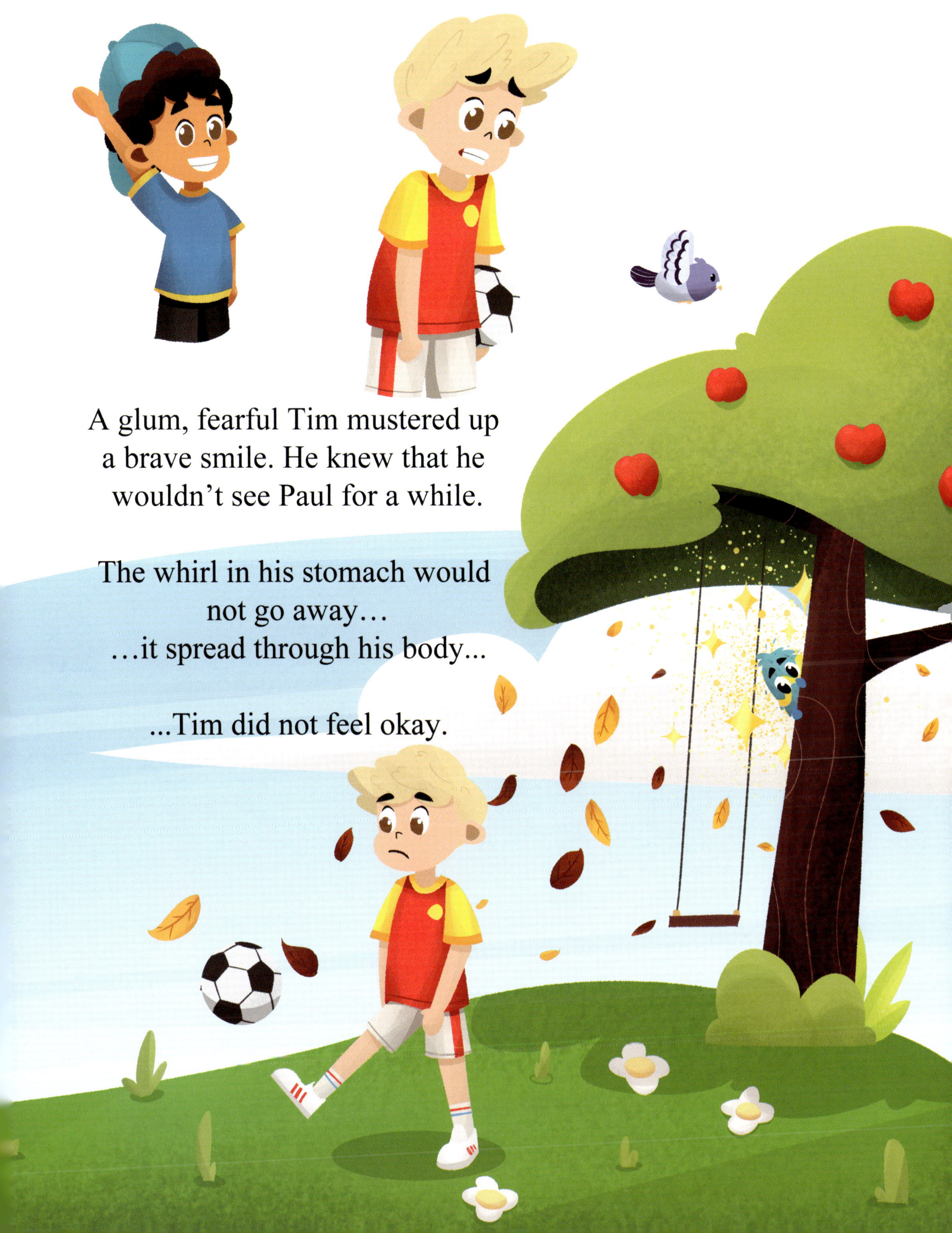

A glum, fearful Tim mustered up
a brave smile. He knew that he
wouldn’t see Paul for a while.

The whirl in his stomach would
not go away…
…it spread through his body...

...Tim did not feel okay.

Before long, the big moving day had arrived.
Tim's mum and dad hauled their cases down the drive.

Tim watched from his old rope swing under the trees.
His head was bent low, he was hugging his knees.

Then suddenly, far in the distance, Tim saw
a mysterious creature he'd not met before.

Striding right up with a grin ear to ear,
was an odd little fellow, but Tim felt no fear.

This fabulous critter was half a foot tall,
his body made up of a tangled fluff ball.

His fur a bold colour of the brightest blue,
with neon zigzags, and stripy socks too.

Dazzling white teeth, a twinkle in his eye,
where did he come from, this strange little guy?

The beastie delved into the fur on his back,
and pulled out a business card, golden and black.

"So, you're here to look after me?
Thank you, but why?"
The creature's eyes sparkled,
but he gave no reply.

"It's time!" shouted mum. "Let's go! Time for the flight!"
The Zuggler crept into Tim's bag out of sight.

Cases packed in the taxi with no time to spare.
Nana Foy saying "Goodbye! You take care!"

YALLA HABIBIS
LET'S GO!

Now at the airport, Tim tried not to cry,
as they boarded an Emirates flight to Dubai.

“To adventures!” said Mr Foy. “Let’s celebrate!
Our new life ahead will be totally great!”

Mrs Foy’s brimming with joy, she’s so happy,
but Tim’s overwhelmed, feeling tired, a bit snappy.

The zip on his backpack opened a tad,
and out shot a ‘thumbs-up’
unseen by his dad.

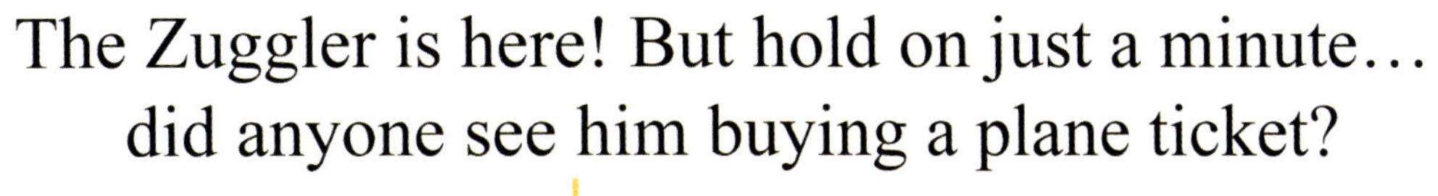

The Zuggler is here! But hold on just a minute…
did anyone see him buying a plane ticket?

The Zuggler

Whenever you find yourself sad or in need,
I will always be with you to help you succeed.

Timothy tucked into fish, chips and peas.
That little thumbs-up made him
feel more at ease.

Tim thought that Dubai was the best place he'd seen.
A city once desert, but now rather green.

Palm trees and bright flowers lining each street,
and beautiful beaches - it was such a new treat.

They all took a trip to sightsee and explore
the mighty Burj Khalifa to the 148th floor!

Surrounded by fountains and a huge shopping mall,
WOW, Dubai is amazing! Not so bad after all!

The Foys settled into their brand-new abode,
a beautiful villa, with a gate - with a code!

“Peace at last”, Tim thought,
sitting alone in his room,
when out of his backpack,
The Zuggler did ZOOM!

He whizzed round the villa at maximum speed,
then stopped and winked at Tim…

…The Zuggler was pleased.

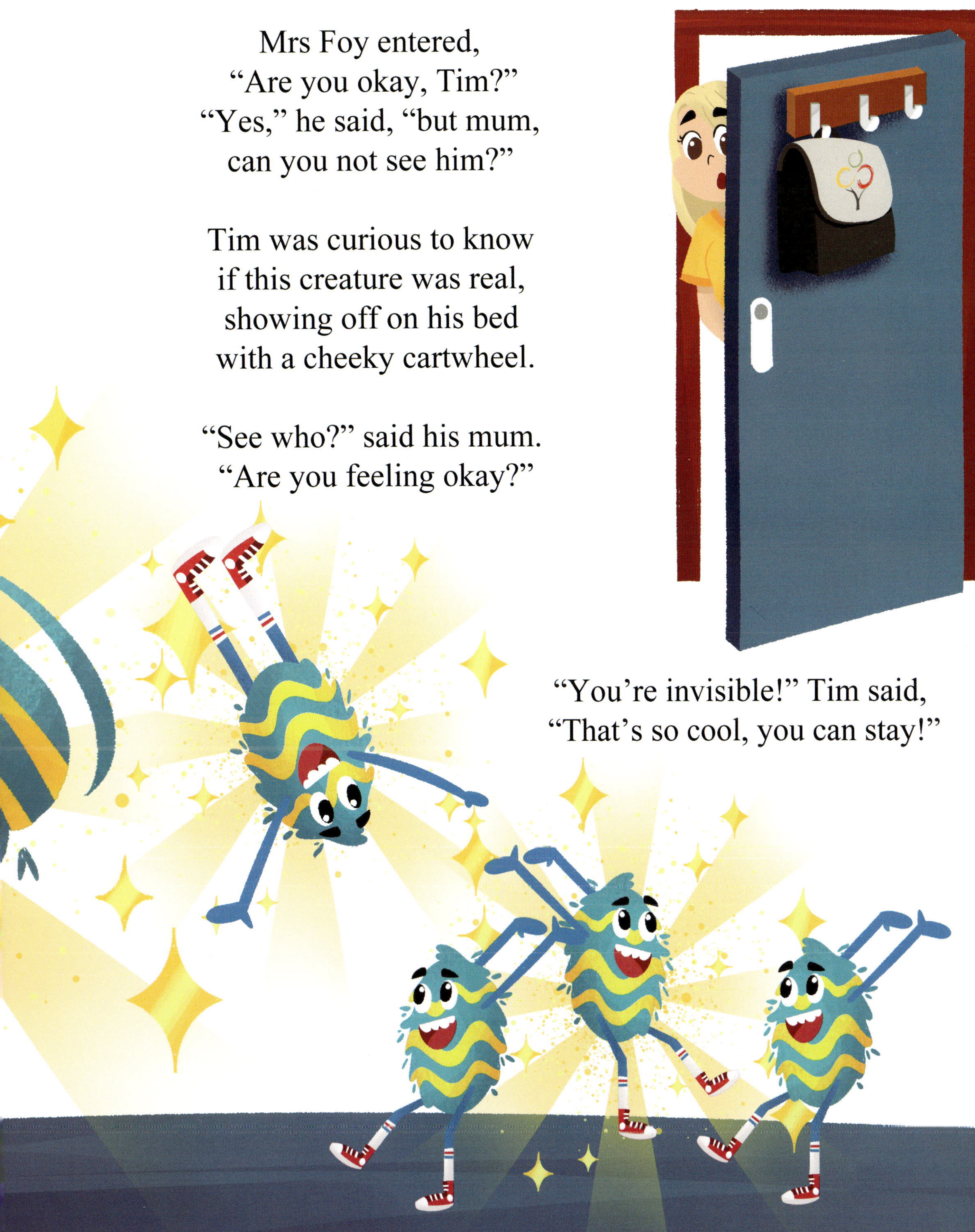

Mrs Foy entered,
"Are you okay, Tim?"
"Yes," he said, "but mum,
can you not see him?"

Tim was curious to know
if this creature was real,
showing off on his bed
with a cheeky cartwheel.

"See who?" said his mum.
"Are you feeling okay?"

"You're invisible!" Tim said,
"That's so cool, you can stay!"

Day one arrived at Timmy's new school,
an impressive building with a theatre and pool.

Greeted by his new teacher with, "Don't worry dear.
My name is Miss Thompson. Come sit over here."

Tim was surprised the kids looked nothing the same:
different skin colours, hairstyles,
and interesting names.

“Here we have pupils of all nationalities,
where cultures unite and
combine with great ease.

Children from Mexico, France, Lebanon,
we speak many languages,
yet our hearts beat as one.”

The children rushed for playtime,
but shy Tim chose to linger.

The Zuggler suddenly appeared,
Paul’s ball spinning on his finger!

The ball caught the attention of two kids from registration.
They glanced at new arrival Tim and knew the situation.

“Hola! My name is Santi, and I am from Brazil.
I like your ball! Let’s have a game, and you can show your skill.”

“Salam!” the second kid said.
“You’re Tim? My name is Reem.
Come play with us, don’t be alone.
We can start a team!”

From that moment on, the three new friends stuck together like glue.

The Zuggler felt very proud as Timothy's confidence grew.

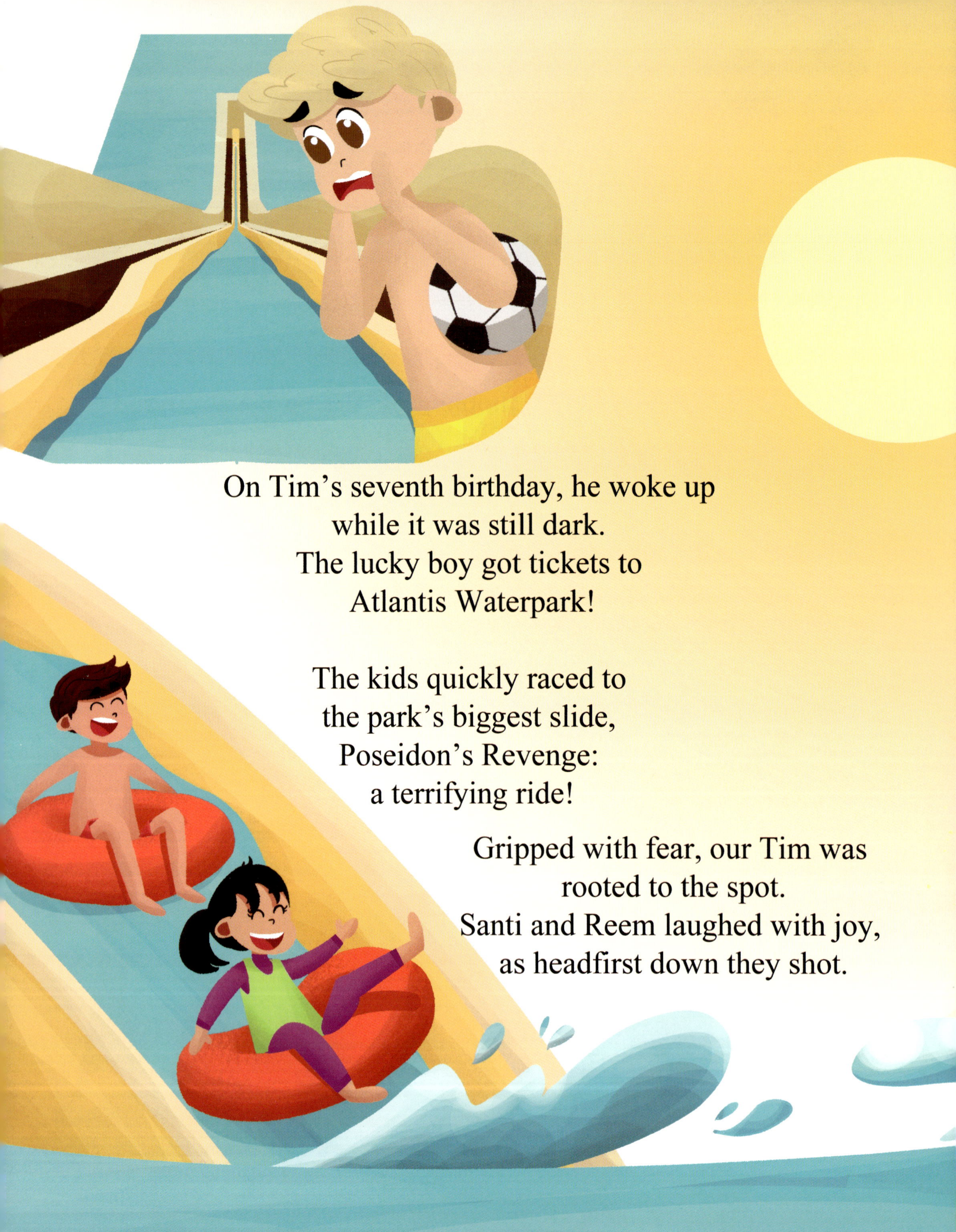

On Tim’s seventh birthday, he woke up
while it was still dark.
The lucky boy got tickets to
Atlantis Waterpark!

The kids quickly raced to
the park’s biggest slide,
Poseidon’s Revenge:
a terrifying ride!

Gripped with fear, our Tim was
rooted to the spot.
Santi and Reem laughed with joy,
as headfirst down they shot.

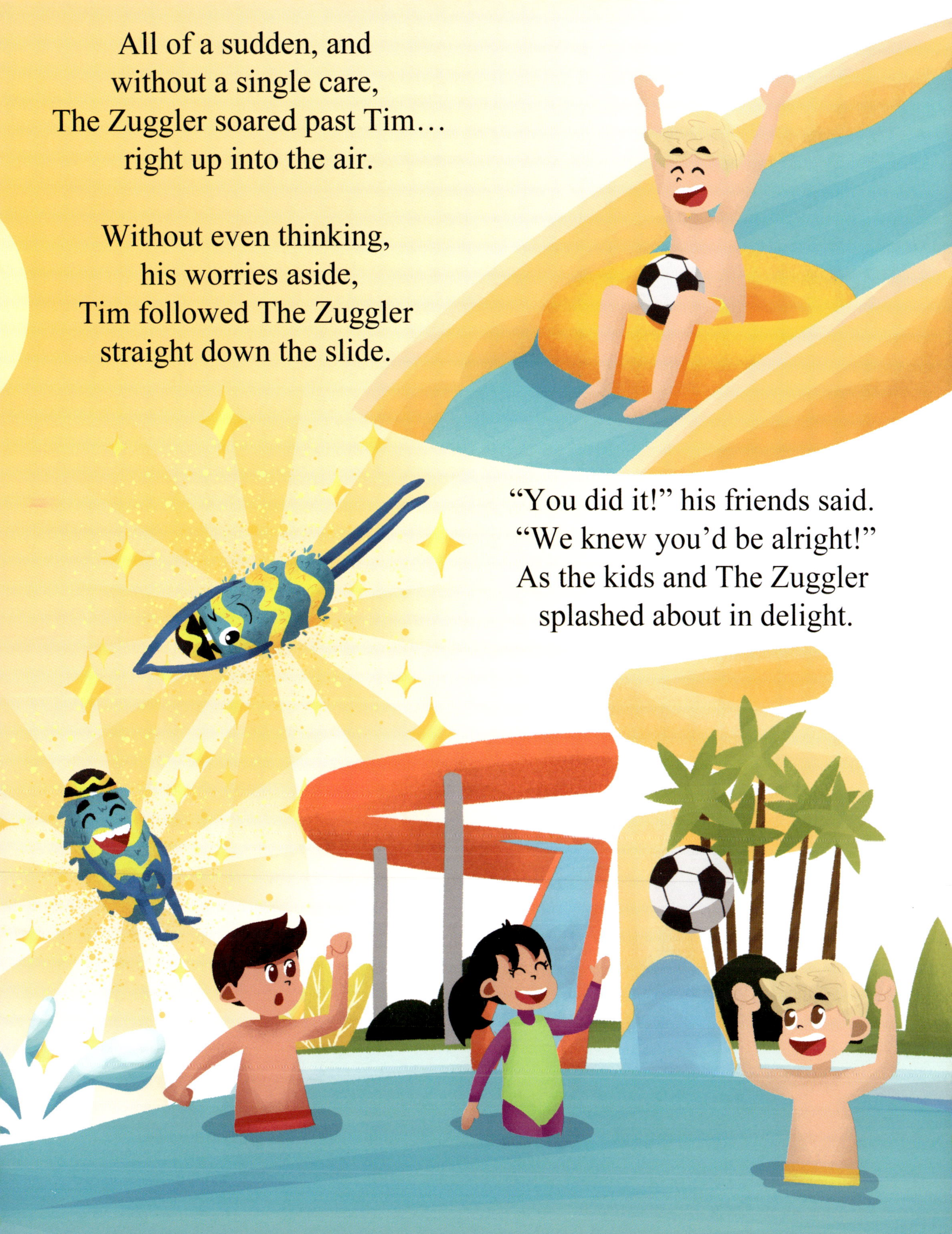

All of a sudden, and
without a single care,
The Zuggler soared past Tim…
right up into the air.

Without even thinking,
his worries aside,
Tim followed The Zuggler
straight down the slide.

"You did it!" his friends said.
"We knew you'd be alright!"
As the kids and The Zuggler
splashed about in delight.

On many occasions over the years,
The Zuggler helped Tim to face his greatest fears.

When the Foys visited the Sheikh Zayed Mosque,
The Zuggler held Tim's hand in case he got lost.

At desert camel riding, he kept Tim really calm.

Guess what, they even skydived -
right over The Palm!

Jet-skiing and ziplining, hours of fun they had.
With The Zuggler by his side, Tim hardly ever felt sad.

One day the phone rang.
Tim's Nana Foy was sick.
The Zuggler tried to comfort Tim
with his best magic trick.

Through the highs and the lows,
The Zuggler was there,
to give Tim support
if things got too much to bear.

As Timothy got older, The Foys moved quite a lot.
They left The UAE and sailed the sea to Kuwait on a yacht.

Onto Saudi Arabia,
a new home in Oman.
Then “goodbye” to the Middle East
and over to Japan.

With The Zuggler by his side,
our Tim could cope with all the change.

He grew, he learned, and knew
he could now handle anything “strange.”

Tim finished school; all exams passed.
No longer a child; a young adult at last.

A confident young man Tim has grown into now.
Well done, The Zuggler, go on, take a bow.

But there's no sign of The Zuggler, nothing, not one…

…and just like that,

The Zuggler...

**...was gone.**